MOTHER
TO THE POOR

The Story of Blessed Teresa of Calcutta

Written by Jung-wook Ko
Illustrated by Seung-bum Park

Pauline
BOOKS & MEDIA
Boston

Library of Congress Cataloging-in-Publication Data
Ko, Jung-wook.
  [Mongdangyeonpili Doen Mother Teresa. English]
  Mother to the poor : the story of Blessed Teresa of Calcutta / written by Jung-wook Ko ;
illustrated by Seung-bum Park.— 1st English ed.
      p. cm.
  ISBN 0-8198-4863-8
  1. Teresa, Mother, 1910-1997. 2. Missionaries of Charity—Biography. 3. Nuns—India—
Calcutta—Biography. I. Park, Seung-bum. II. Title.
  BX4406.5.Z8K6213 2008
  271'.97—dc22

                        2007046007

Originally published in Korea by Pauline Books & Media, 103 Mia 9-dong, Gangbuk-gu, Seoul 142-704 Korea

Original edition title: *Mongdangyeonpili Doen Mother Teresa*

Translated from Korean by Mary W. Chung

English adaptation by Diane M. Lynch

First English edition, 2008

Published by Pauline Books & Media, 50 Saint Pauls Avenue, Boston, MA 02130-3491

Printed in Korea

www.pauline.org

Pauline Books & Media is the publishing house of the Daughters of St. Paul, an international congregation of women religious serving the Church with the communications media.

For the location of the Pauline Books & Media Center nearest you,
please visit www.pauline.org.

1 2 3 4 5 6 7 8 9   12 11 10 09 08

CONTENTS

Dear Readers,

Have you ever noticed homeless people on a city street? Maybe you've watched the news on TV or read headlines on the Internet. The news may be about wars, famines, and floods. It may be about tidal waves and hurricanes. There are so many people who need help!

How could just one person ever make a difference?

Mother Teresa saw a lot of problems in the world. She was just one small person, but she decided to roll up her sleeves and help. She began with love. She followed Jesus' teachings to feed the hungry, give drink to the thirsty, welcome the stranger, clothe the naked, and visit the sick. She and her sisters worked to weave a chain of love around the world.

Because of Mother Teresa, thousands of poor people, both children and adults, have been able to live better lives. Although Annie, the child in this story, is not real, she represents many children helped by Mother Teresa and the Missionaries of Charity. I hope you enjoy meeting both the make-believe Annie and the real Mother Teresa in this book.

Jung-wook Ko
Suwon, Korea

"Truly I tell you, just as you did it to one of the least of these who are members of my family, you did it to me" (Matthew 25:40).

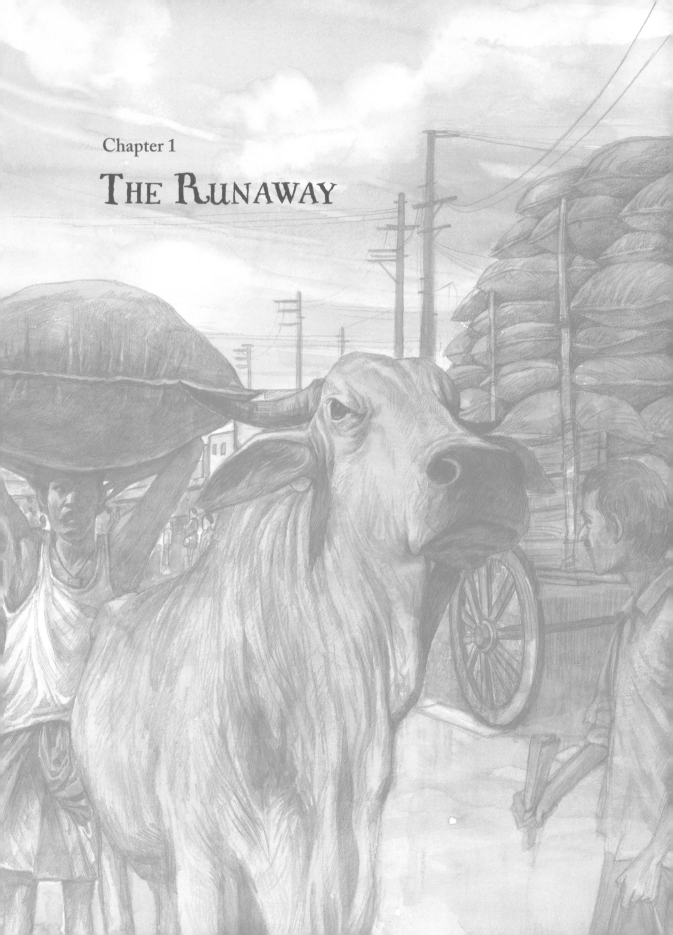

Chapter 1

THE RUNAWAY

Kalighat Street is one of the busiest streets in Calcutta, India. Calcutta is a very large city. Its unpaved roads are filled with dust and noise and all kinds of animals: dogs, horses, and even cows. People crowd the streets day and night, bumping into one another as they try to avoid being hit by the cars, motorcycles, wagons, and bicycles that are everywhere. The streets of Calcutta are always full of busy people.

Twelve million people live in Calcutta. The old section of the city—the northern part—is one of the poorest areas. This part of Calcutta is very crowded and dirty. One day, two Catholic sisters, one elderly and one young, walked quickly through the streets. The older sister was short and bent over. Deep wrinkles lined her face. Her sari—a special type of Indian dress—was so worn out that she could have been mistaken for a beggar.

The sisters stopped at a small fruit and vegetable stand.

"Do you know a girl named Annie?" the older one asked the shop owner.

Just then a passing cow leaned down and began munching on one of the piled-up apples. The mustached shop owner chased the cow away, answering the sister at the same time.

"What a question, Sister! There are so many wandering and abandoned children out on the streets. How would I know who Annie is?"

The sisters thanked the man and kept on walking. The older woman looked closely at every child they passed. She walked quickly but carefully, trying to avoid the rubbish in the streets.

"Where are you, Annie?" she kept calling. "Where are you?"

Suddenly, the younger sister shouted, "Mother, there she is!"

The elderly sister ran to the spot. A little girl was sitting very still by the side of the road.

"Annie, we finally found you!" the older woman exclaimed with joy. "What happened? Didn't you like our Children's Home? Did we do something wrong?"

Annie shook her head and smiled shyly.

"I liked the home a lot," she whispered, "but my mother is here."

The sister turned around. She saw a woman wrapped in a torn blanket lying nearby. The woman looked very sick. Beside her was a tin pot. The sister understood. *Annie and her mother beg on the streets for food. They heat it in the pot. It's all they have…*

For a moment, the sister couldn't say a word. She felt as though her heart would break. She made the sign of the cross and said a prayer for Annie and her mother.

Her thoughts went back to the week before, when she had found Annie lying in the street. The little girl had been starving. She had been very dirty and ragged.

Annie had weighed so little that the sister had been able to carry her in her arms to the Children's Home. There the sisters had given her food, bathed her, and dressed her in clean clothes. Soon Annie had started to look healthier. But her face had remained very sad.

That very morning, Annie had disappeared. The starving, poor, and neglected children living at the Home usually wanted to stay as long as possible. The sisters couldn't understand why Annie had run away.

"My mother is here," Annie explained. "I can't live without my mother!"

The sisters saw the joy on Annie's face. They understood she was happy to be with her mother—even if it meant being homeless, living on the filthy street, and having to beg for food. "I must stay with my mother," the little girl insisted.

14

The younger sister whispered something to the older one. The elderly sister replied, "After all, we all need our mothers' love." She bent down and took the thin hand of Annie's mother.

"You are very ill," she said kindly. "Let us take you to our Missionary of Charity House."

"I can't move," the woman answered in a weak voice.

"Don't worry," the sister replied. "We're going to help you. We're going to carry you on a stretcher."

The young sister hurried back to the convent. She soon returned with another sister and a stretcher.

"We're going to take care of you and Annie," the elderly sister told the woman. "You don't have to worry anymore."

The sisters carried Annie's mother back to their Home. Annie walked happily alongside Mother Teresa, the elderly sister whose whole life was spent in helping and serving the poorest of the poor.

Chapter 2

A HAPPY LIFE

After Annie returned to the Children's Home, known as *Shishu Bhavan,* she quickly began to gain weight. Annie's mother, too, was glad to be there. Because of the clean surroundings and good food, her health improved. The volunteer doctors visited her regularly and gave her medicine that helped her sickness.

Life was much happier for Annie.

"Sister Maria!" Annie called to her friend, the sister who had helped Mother Teresa rescue Annie and her mother.

"Annie, are you still feeling dizzy?" Sister Maria asked. "Are you any better?"

"I'm fine now, Sister. It was just the hunger that made me feel so sick."

"I'm so glad, Annie. God was truly with us the day we found you!"

"What are you carrying, Sister?" Annie asked. "Can I help you?"

"Yes, Annie. I'm taking these clothes and supplies to the babies' nursery. You can come, too!"

Annie helped Sister Maria carry the neatly folded clothes down the hall to the nursery.

In the nursery, volunteers from Korea, Australia, and Japan were helping sisters to care for the children. Annie gathered the babies' dirty clothes and heaped them in the large tin laundry bucket to be washed.

The weather was hot that day, as it usually is in India. A bead of perspiration ran down Annie's nose and dropped into the laundry bucket.

My goodness, it's hot! Annie thought. She wiped the water from her face and listened to the hum of a distant fan blowing steamy air.

I'll be fine…at least here we have a fan. The sisters don't have any in their convent. They want to live as humbly as the poorest of the poor, as humbly as Jesus did…Jesus didn't have a fan, either!

Annie finished piling the dirty clothes in the bucket and stooped to play with one of the babies. Then she heard a kind voice.

"Annie, what a good girl you are!"

All the volunteers and helpers stopped to greet Mother Teresa, who smiled at them and motioned that they should go on working.

"Annie, is the work too hard for you?"

"Oh, no, Mother," Annie replied. "I love helping, and I love playing with the babies! Before, because we were so poor, I never thought I'd be able to help other children. But here at the Home, we older children take care of the younger ones. It's like having lots and lots of brothers and sisters!"

Mother Teresa smiled and touched Annie's cheek. "And how is your mother, Annie?"

"She's getting better, Mother."

"That is good, very good."

"But…Mother, I have something to ask you."

"What is it?" Mother Teresa asked kindly.

Annie hesitated for a moment, then made up her mind.

"Even when my mother is well, will I be able to stay and help with the babies?" she asked, her eyes shining with hope.

Mother Teresa smiled at Annie's eagerness. "Yes, my child, of course you'll be able to stay. We love you and we need your help—and your mother's, too, when she gets better!"

"Really?"

"Yes, really!"

"Oh, thank you, Mother! I'll work very hard."

Mother Teresa watched thoughtfully as Annie pushed the bucketful of soiled clothes into the laundry room. Annie reminded her of another little girl long, long ago. *When I was Annie's age,* she thought, *I, too, always dreamed about helping others…*

***

"Gonxha!"

Father was home unusually early that day.

"Where are you, my little Gonxha? I have a gift for you!"

His young daughter came running.

"My darling daughter, have you been a good girl? This is for you."

"What is it, Papa?" Gonxha asked as she tore excitedly at the wrapping paper.

Inside was the most adorable stuffed bear!

"Oh, thank you, Papa. I love it!" A hug and a kiss were this loving father's reward.

 Agnes Gonxha Bojaxhiu was born on August 26, 1910, in Skopje (pronounced SKOP-yeh), a small town in Macedonia in a region that was formerly part of Albania. Later the area would become part of Yugoslavia. She was the youngest of three children. Her father, Nikola, and her mother, Dranafile, often called her by her middle name, Gonxha (pronounced GOHN-jay). It means "flower bud."

The Bojaxhiu family was Catholic, and Agnes had a deep faith and trust in God throughout her childhood. Her parents taught her to pray. One of the joys of Agnes's life was the family's weekly trip to Sunday Mass.

Nikola Bojaxhiu was a leading figure in Skopje. He was a member of the town council as well as a successful merchant. He worked hard and was always busy, but never too busy to help people in need. His family lived in a big house surrounded by a beautiful garden full of flowers, shrubs, and fruit trees.

But this peaceful and happy life was about to change.

One day when Agnes was eight years old, her father left home to attend a political gathering in Belgrade, a city about 160 miles from Skopje.

Suddenly, late that night, there was loud pounding on the door. Mrs. Bojaxhiu flew to answer it.

"Mrs. Bojaxhiu!" gasped the man at the door. "Your husband collapsed at the meeting. He's very ill. We think he's been poisoned!"

Nikola was rushed to the hospital, where he underwent surgery. In spite of his family's hopes and prayers, he died the next day.

Life would not be easy for the young widow and her children. Now that her husband was gone, there was very little money. How would Mrs. Bojaxhiu feed, clothe, and educate three children?

"Almighty God, I put my trust in you," she prayed. "I know you will give me the grace and the strength I need. Help me to raise my children well. Help me to teach them to love you above all. Your will be done."

Soon the young widow realized she would have to start earning money. She began a small business, sewing and selling clothing. Slowly at first, customers started to appear.

The little family prayed together each night. After school, the children helped their mother. Agnes swept the floor and dusted the tables. Her brother, Lazar, ran errands and made deliveries. Aga, her older sister, helped with the sewing.

Poor people often came to ask for used clothing for their children. Warmhearted Mrs. Bojaxhiu never let them leave empty-handed. Often she invited her poorer neighbors to share the family meal.

"My dears," she told Agnes, Lazar, and Aga, "all people are our brothers and sisters. We are all children of God."

One evening, the little family sat in their living room. The three children worked at their homework. Lazar finished the paper he was working on and clapped his book closed.

"Done at last! Aga, you should have seen what John's brother did today in class! What a fool!"

"What?" asked Aga. "And then I have something funny to tell you about Barbara—you won't believe it!"

As the children talked and laughed, Mrs. Bojaxhiu continued to sew. Finally she quietly got up and left the room. Just as Lazar was snickering at Aga's story, the lights suddenly went out.

A moment later, Mrs. Bojaxhiu was at the door.

"Mother! What's going on?" the children demanded.

"My dear children, I've just turned off the main electric switch. Tell me, do you think it's right to talk about people this way? Electricity is very expensive, you know, and we're not going to waste it so you can gossip and call people names. If unkind things are all you have to talk about, then the lights will stay off!"

Lazar, Aga, and Agnes were silent.

"Think of the many people who are so poor they have nothing," continued Mrs. Bohjaxhiu. "We're lucky to have a comfortable home and enough to eat, and even enough to share. We certainly aren't wasting any of our blessings, including electricity, for such a foolish purpose."

Agnes thought about her mother's words. She remembered the many poor children she saw each day as she walked home from school.

"You're right, Mother. We've been selfish, and we need to do more! How can we help?"

Mrs. Bojaxhiu smiled at her eager daughter. "We'll pray. You can be sure that God will show us the way!"

Mrs. Bojaxhiu's faith inspired her children. The next day, the family joined a group of pilgrims visiting the chapel of Our Lady of Letnice on the slopes of Skopje's Black Mountain. Together they knelt and prayed until late in the evening. This was the first of many visits Agnes would make to the chapel.

One day at their parish church, the two sisters met a group of people who were there to attend a missionary meeting. They were praying for missionaries around the world and hoped to become missionaries themselves.

"Missionaries?" Agnes asked. "What kind of work would you do?"

"We want to go to other countries to help less fortunate people by building hospitals and orphanages. We want to bring the Good News of Jesus to them!"

This gave Agnes a lot to think about.

Could I become a missionary someday? she wondered. *I want to be like my parents, and they've always helped the poor. But how will I know? Will God send me a sign?*

Father Jambrekovic, the parish priest, encouraged Agnes to attend the missionary meetings regularly.

"Of course God will send a sign," Father told her. "Your joy in helping others will point you to what God wants!"

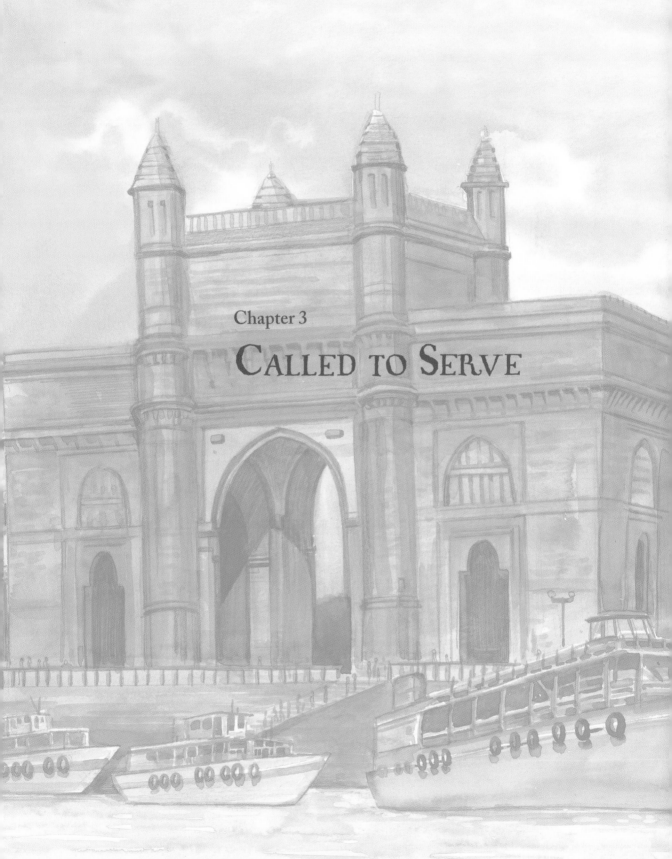

Chapter 3

CALLED TO SERVE

One Sunday, church bells rang out through the town. As people streamed from the church and headed home, only Agnes remained. As she always did after Mass, she knelt down to pray before the statue of the Blessed Mother.

As she prayed, she suddenly heard a voice in her heart.

"Agnes, dedicate your life to Jesus Christ. Become a religious sister and serve the Lord through serving the poor."

34

Agnes had thought and prayed about her vocation. For some time, she had been sure that God wanted her to work among the poor. Before this moment, however, she had never thought about entering religious life and becoming a sister.

When she heard the inner voice, she was convinced. *This calling is from God,* she thought. *My heart is singing. I will serve you and your people joyously, Lord!*

Agnes stood and gazed at the statue of the Blessed Mother. She could feel Mary's tender and loving embrace.

"Oh, Holy Mother! Thank you, thank you. What joy to serve God!"

For the next few years, Agnes kept her vocation to herself. She continued to attend the parish meetings for

missionaries. Occasionally, missionary priests and sisters living around the world sent newsletters about the work they were doing. Agnes was sure she would someday be called to Africa. But one day she was drawn to the letters and photographs sent from India.

Here are people who are the poorest of the poor, she thought. *I believe God is calling me to India.*

In 1928, when Agnes was eighteen years old, she decided the time had come to open her heart. She would tell her mother about her vocation.

"Mother, I want to be a religious sister and join the Loreto Sisters, the Irish branch of the Institute of the Blessed Virgin Mary. They work with the Jesuits in Bengal, India. God has called me to serve the poor there."

Mrs. Bojaxhiu wasn't surprised. She had wondered for some time whether Agnes would want to enter a religious congregation. She hesitated, but not because she didn't approve of the idea. She wanted to be sure her daughter really understood the importance of this step.

"Agnes, if you become a sister, you'll never be able to

live with our family again. You might not even be able to visit us, especially if you are sent to a country far away. Are you sure this is what you want?"

Agnes smiled. "I understand, Mother. Just as I love you, Lazar, and Aga, I want to love and serve all of God's people."

Mrs. Bojaxhiu couldn't give Agnes an answer right away. "I must think about this," she told her daughter.

Agnes's mother went to her bedroom and quietly closed the door. For hours, she prayed and asked God to know his will.

Suddenly she knew the answer.

Mrs. Bohaxhiu came out of her room with a little smile on her face.

"You have my blessing. Dear Lord, guide and protect Agnes!"

She embraced Agnes and kissed her, and they both wept.

"Agnes, this is indeed God's will. We'll miss you so much. But I know you will be only, and all, for Jesus!"

On August 15, 1928, the feast of the Assumption, Agnes joined the parish pilgrimage to Our Lady of Letnice for the last time. No one knows exactly what her thoughts and prayers were that day. We can be sure, though, that she asked for the help and guidance of our Blessed Mother in her new life.

The next day, she boarded a train to Zagreb. Almost a hundred friends and family members were at the train station to wave goodbye. How Agnes would miss them all, but how excited she was to begin her new life!

On October 12, after a stop in Paris, Agnes and a companion, Betika Kajnc, reached Dublin, Ireland. Together they were accepted into the congregation of the Sisters of Loreto.

Agnes and Betika stayed only six weeks in Dublin. Most of their time was spent in learning English. They also learned a great deal about Indian history and culture, because they would soon be sent to begin their work in that huge country.

In December, the two young women boarded a ship

for India. A month later, the ship steamed past Bombay harbor. After a stormy voyage and stops at Colombo and Madras, they arrived at the bustling port city of Calcutta.

"India, at last!" Agnes exclaimed.

From her first moment in Calcutta, Agnes loved the people and the city. It was very hot, and the smells in the dusty streets weren't always pleasant, but that didn't bother the young postulant. Her heart was happy. She would soon begin her mission of serving the people of India!

India, Agnes knew, was one of the world's oldest civilizations. It was an enormous land surrounded by mountains and plateaus, and had a very large population. At that time, the country was still ruled by England. Many of the Indian people were very poor.

Agnes and Betika stayed in Calcutta for only one week. Then they traveled by train to the Loreto convent in Darjeeling, in the foothills of the mighty Himalayas. For two years, the young novices learned about the work of the Loreto Sisters and were taught all about religious

life. They also learned Hindi and Bengali, two important languages of India.

On March 24, 1931, Agnes made her first vows as a Loreto Sister. Her new religious name was Sister Mary Teresa. From then on, she would be known simply as Sister Teresa.

Not long after Sister Teresa made her vows, Mother Superior called her into her office.

"Sister Teresa, we think you have a talent for teaching. We would like you to teach at Saint Mary's School, part of our Entally convent in Calcutta. We know you will do your very best for the students there."

Sister Teresa smiled with joy. "Yes, Mother Superior. Thank you!"

Teaching made Teresa very happy. She wasn't much older than some of her students. Many thought of her as an older sister! But outside the walls of the school compound, she realized, there were big problems. There was great poverty and many children who needed help. Sister Teresa encouraged her pupils to join the Sodality of the Blessed Virgin. Girls who joined the Sodality spent weekends visiting poor families, often bringing gifts for the children.

On May 24, 1937, Sister Teresa made her final vows as a Loreto Sister. As usual in the Loreto congregation, she was called "Mother Teresa" from that time on. In addition to teaching at the high school, she was put in charge of Saint Teresa's Primary School. Mother Teresa was busier than ever!

But there was little peace in India. World War II was soon raging, and the country was caught in the conflict. The British military took over the transportation system. During the war, India could not transport rice from Burma to feed its millions of citizens. Starving people in rural areas fled to Calcutta, hoping for food. Thousands died in the streets every day. The Great Famine claimed the lives of over two million Indians.

By 1945, the war had ended, but there were even more problems in store. In August of 1946, riots broke out in Calcutta. The city became a battleground as

Hindus and Muslims each fought to take over the city. In the conflict, thousands more people died.

Mother Teresa was in charge of Saint Mary's School at the time. Because of the violence in the streets, no food was available. Mother Teresa was responsible for 300 hungry girls.

"We must to do something! We cannot let them die!" she told her sisters.

So, alone, Mother Teresa went out into the streets of Calcutta looking for enough food to feed her students. She was stopped by army troops, who drove her back to the school…with enough bags of rice to feed the entire school!

The sisters always ate as little as possible so the children would have more food, and soon Mother Teresa became very weak.

Mother Superior, worried about Teresa's health, decided this would be a good time for her to go on retreat. She would go to the sisters' house in Darjeeling, 400 miles away. On September 10, 1946, Mother Teresa made her way through the dusty streets of Calcutta to the train station. As she walked, she saw the suffering, the sickness, and the hunger. On the train, she could not forget the misery of the poor.

Clickety-clack, clickety-clack, clickety-clack, clattered the wheels on the tracks.

And that was when she heard the inner voice.

"Teresa! Leave the Loreto convent and school, and help the poor and the needy while living among them."

She knew the voice was the voice of God, and she prayed, "Dear Lord, please give me the strength and the power to devote my life to the poorest of the poor."

During that train journey, on the day now known as "Inspiration Day," Mother understood that God had called her to do very special work. She knew that, with his help, she would somehow find a way to answer his call.

Chapter 4

THE POOREST
OF THE POOR

During her retreat in Darjeeling, Mother Teresa rested and became healthier. When the retreat was over, she began to plan how to help the poor people in the slums of Calcutta. Mother was ready to do anything and to suffer anything for Jesus.

She knew God was calling her to live among the poor, but she also felt that he wanted her to remain a religious sister. She would have to leave the Loreto Sisters to start a new congregation to live and work in the slums. But how would all this happen? She asked her spiritual advisor, Father Celeste Van Exem, for guidance.

One day, someone knocked on the front door of Archbishop Périer's house. When the archbishop opened the door, he found Mother Teresa standing there.

"Oh, Mother Teresa," he smiled. "Please come in."

After Mother Teresa greeted Archbishop Périer, they sat down on the couch.

"How was your retreat, Mother?"

"It was very good, Your Excellency."

The archbishop was puzzled.

"Do you have some problem to discuss?"

"Archbishop Périer, I've seen so many poor people suffering for such a long time. Ever since I was young, I've wanted to help them, but I didn't know how. While I was on retreat, I heard a call from God. He said, 'Leave everything and live with the poor people and help them.' He wants me to begin a new congregation of sisters to help the people who are the poorest of the poor. The people who have no one else."

The archbishop didn't know what to say. How could he be sure this was really God's plan for Mother Teresa?

"Mother, I cannot give any answer right away. If you stay and teach children, you will be helping poor people. You may serve the poor by serving children."

Mother Teresa was not to be stopped.

"No, I must live with the poorest of people and I must live as they live. After all, Jesus told the rich young man, 'Go and sell all you have and give the money to the poor, and then follow me.' "

The archbishop thought. "Mother Teresa, living and working in the slums of the city will be dangerous and hard. Can you do it?"

"Yes. Please help me. I have taken my final vows. To leave the Loreto Sisters, I have to get approval from our Mother General and from the Vatican. Archbishop Périer, I need your help and advice."

"And you will get it, Mother, but not right away. First we must be sure that this is really the right thing to do."

The archbishop kept his word. For more than a year, Mother Teresa worked at the Entally convent and then at the convent in Asansol. Finally she received permission to write to Mother Gertrude, the Mother General of her congregation in Ireland. She asked to leave the Loreto convent in order to live and work among the poor in Calcutta.

On February 2, 1948, Mother Gertrude wrote back to say yes!

Now it was time to write to the Vatican, the headquarters of the Catholic Church in Rome. Mother Teresa said a prayer and began her letter.

Dear Holy Father,

My name is Mother Teresa, and I am of the Loreto Sisters in India. For many years, I have taught children at our school, and I have obeyed God's will. I have heard a second calling from God to offer myself for the service of the poorest of the poor in the slums. So many people are dying on the streets in Calcutta without getting any help! It is God's will that I go to live among them and help them, as Jesus would do.

I am asking permission to leave the Loreto Sisters and to live and work with these poorest of people. I trust God fully, and humbly request Your Holiness to grant me the permission for my work as well as your blessing.

Mother Teresa
Loreto Sisters

The letter went to the Vatican in Rome, Italy. A meeting was held at the Vatican. There was a great deal of discussion about whether or not to agree to the sister's plan.

"Mother Teresa's requests and ideas are most unusual," said one priest. "When a sister takes her final vows, she is bound to live in the convent and follow the rules of the congregation."

Most of the advisors wanted to refuse Mother Teresa's request, but a few of them disagreed.

"The convent is a place to live and act on God's word," said one. "But why should we be against a different calling to serve God? Mother Teresa's plan is to give service to the poorest of the poor. She wants to live as they live. Who are we to say no?"

"It's not right," argued another. "If we accept this sister's plan, what if other women want to become sisters to do the same thing? What will happen then?"

"What's the matter with that?" was the response. "More sisters would mean more people living unselfish lives and serving others. Won't that make the world a better place?"

Meanwhile, in Calcutta, Mother Teresa waited, worked, and prayed. When would the answer come? The matter was, she knew, in God's hands.

Chapter 5

THE MISSION BEGINS

One afternoon in July, Archbishop Périer visited the convent.

"Mother Teresa, it's here!" he exclaimed. "The letter from Rome is here!"

Mother Teresa began to read:

For a long time, we have discussed Mother Teresa's plans. Working with the poor and the hopeless, loving them as ourselves, is following in the footsteps of Jesus.

We hereby grant permission for Mother Teresa to leave the convent of the congregation of the Sisters of Loreto in order to live with and serve the poorest of the poor in Calcutta.

As soon as Mother Teresa finished reading the letter, she knelt down and prayed. She gave thanks to God.

"Dear Lord! Thank you, Lord. Please lead me and guide me. You are my Shepherd. I trust your call."

Saying goodbye to the Loreto convent was very hard for Mother Teresa. She realized that she was afraid. It was a great sacrifice to leave the sisters and the children. She had lived and worked for a long time at Loreto, and she loved it there. Now she would be living alone with no one to help or support her.

Suddenly she felt the temptation to stay. She knelt and spoke to God the words that were in her heart.

"Lord, you alone are my support. I trust in your call. I know you will not let me down."

After praying, Teresa got up and went to her room.

"Will Mother Teresa leave everything here? What will she take with her?" wondered the sisters.

Soon Mother came out of her room wearing a cheap, white sari with three blue stripes. She had bought three of the saris at a local market. On her left shoulder was pinned a crucifix. She was carrying her old habits and extra clothing.

"I'll leave these here with you," she told the sisters. "I won't need them now."

The Loreto sisters and all the children cried as Mother Teresa walked down the hill to the office of Mother Superior.

"You are welcome back here anytime…whenever the cross becomes too heavy to bear," said Mother Superior. "We will always be here for you."

"Yes!" cried the others. "We'll miss you. We want to be sure we'll see you again!"

"Thank you, dearest sisters," said Mother Teresa. "You will find me in the city streets among the poor, the ones who have no one else to love them."

Mother Teresa left the Loreto convent and traveled to Patna. There she asked the Medical Missionary Sisters at the Holy Family Hospital to give her some training in nursing.

"Sisters, I came to see you because I need your help. I am going to serve the poorest of the poor in the city. I need to have enough medical training to work there. Please teach me."

The Missionary Sisters were impressed at this dedication.

"Mother Teresa, we will give you all the help we can."

For three months, Mother stayed at the hospital and learned basic nursing. She learned to clean and bandage wounds, give medicines, and care for the dying.

One day, she was talking to one of the sister-doctors.

"I will live in the poorest part of the city and be truly one of the poor," she told her. "I will live as the people do, with only rice and salt to eat."

The doctor frowned.

"If you try to eat only rice and salt, Mother, you won't be living with the poor...you'll be dying with them!" she told her.

Mother Teresa knew she was right.

"I'll remember that, Sister," she said humbly. "I won't

eat more than I need…but I promise I won't eat less, either."

Finally the Medical Missionary Sisters agreed that Mother Theresa was ready to return to Calcutta and begin her work. Her next job was to find somewhere to live.

The Little Sisters of the Poor, who cared for elderly people at Saint Joseph's Home, said that Mother Teresa could live with them. She would be able to go to Mass and eat breakfast each morning before leaving for the slums to do her work. For the first few days, she helped the sisters care for their elderly patients and spent the afternoons in prayer and meditation.

Finally, in December 1948, Mother Teresa left her small room, went to Mass, and then took a bus to the slum of Motijihl. The din of the streets hurt her ears, and the smell was unbearable. Mobs of dirty children begged in the roads. Motionless bodies lay in filthy water in ditches. People, thin as skeletons, searched through trash bins. They were hoping to find food.

"Dear Lord! I came here to fulfill your calling. Give me strength and hope. Help me to give these poor people your love and affection."

After her prayer, Mother Teresa was filled with energy.

"I know what to do! To escape poverty, children must be educated. I'll start a little school and teach them." Mother Teresa visited as many poor families as she could and told them her plan. They promised to send their children to her.

The next morning, children gathered around Mother Teresa. The school had begun. But there was no money for books, chalkboards, desks, or even a school building. How could a school operate without supplies?

"Look, we'll write here. In the mud between the huts!" Mother Teresa bent and began scratching the letters of the Bengali alphabet into the dirt with a stick.

And that was the beginning of the little school. To prevent sickness, Mother Teresa taught the children to wash their hands and keep themselves clean.

"Cleanliness comes first, children. When we are clean, germs don't spread!"

Gradually, as word spread about what Mother was doing, some people began to donate money. Finally she was able to rent two small huts. One would serve as a classroom for the children. The other became a home for poor people who were sick and dying.

At the little school, the children were given food, milk, and prizes for good schoolwork. The prizes were bars of soap!

Soon people started noticing what Mother Teresa was doing. Word spread through Calcutta about the Catholic sister who fed the poor, gave them clean clothing, and ran a school. People donated small gifts: a table, some old stools, even books and slates. Before long, Mother had over fifty students.

But there was more work to be done. God had asked her to found a new congregation of sisters to help the poor. But how could she begin a congregation without a convent? Where would the sisters live?

Chapter 6

A Chain of Love

In the Indian tradition, many people believe they will be blessed if they help the poor. Mother Teresa found herself with quite a few volunteers: Christians, Hindus, Muslims, Jews, and Buddhists. They were willing to donate food and money. They also offered to help her teach in the school and to care for the sick and dying.

Mother Teresa knew she would need even more helpers. Whenever she had time, she wrote letters to thank people for their help. She also wrote about how much more help was needed.

One day, Mother sat down to write a letter. She was using a pencil that had been sharpened and sharpened until it was only a little stub.

God is using me to do his work, she thought. *I'm like a tiny pencil in the hand of God! Dear Lord, I pray you will let me do your work until I am as small as this pencil.*

The search for a house for the new congregation went on. Mother Teresa looked throughout the city. Finally, Father Van Exem spoke to a family with a house on Creek Lane. The owners offered to let Mother live in a room on the second floor of the house rent-free. Mother Teresa happily said yes!

In the beginning, Mother didn't have much furniture. She had only a bench, a box to use as a table, a chair given to her by the Little Sisters of the Poor, and a bed sent by the Sisters of Loreto. A picture of Our Lady of Fatima rested on a little green cupboard. Mother Teresa, as always, placed her trust in God and in the Blessed Mother.

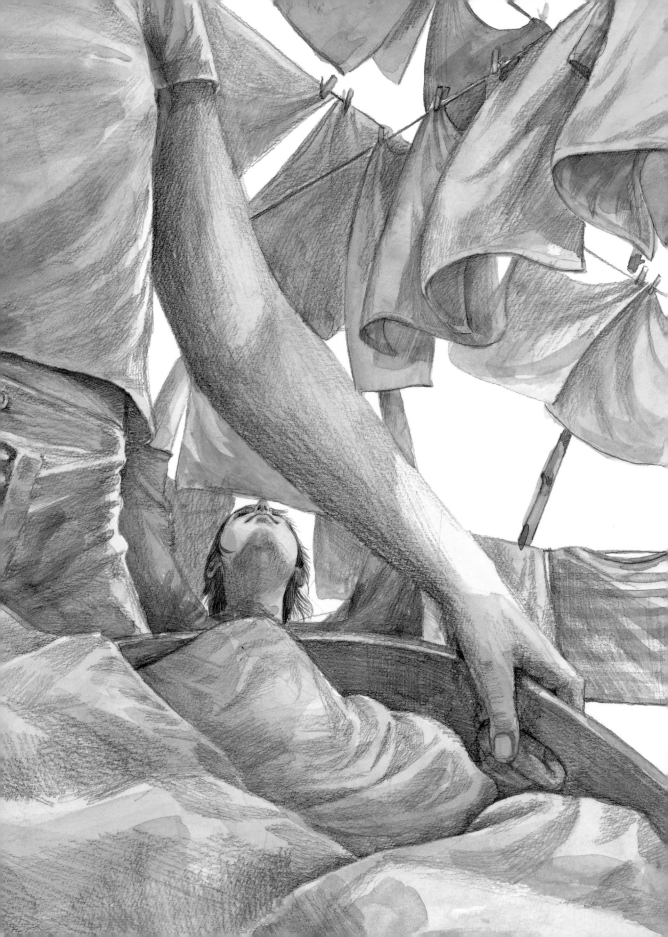

One day there was a knock on the door. A young Bengali woman stood outside.

"Mother Teresa, it's me, Subhasini Das! I was your pupil at the convent school. Do you remember me?"

"Dear Subhasini, of course I do. What brings you here?"

"I've graduated from school. I want to join you in your work, Mother. I hope to become a sister, like you."

"Subhasini, it will not be an easy life," Mother Teresa answered. "There will be many problems and much hardship ahead. Are you sure?"

"Mother! Please accept me. Please don't ask me to go back. My decision comes from the bottom of my heart."

"Then I do accept you, Subhasini. And I welcome you from the bottom of *my* heart!"

Subhasini was the first to join Mother Teresa. Eventually, she would become Sister Agnes. One by one, more of Mother's former students made their way to the house on Creek Lane. Soon there were eleven young Bengali women living at the convent. With their help, a second school was opened.

Mother Teresa and her sisters lived in real poverty. They did their washing in tin buckets. They had two spare saris apiece. Each owned one tin plate, one cup, a light blanket, a crucifix, a rosary, and one pair of sandals. To them, the most important thing was begging for the poor. They weren't concerned with their own needs.

Mother Teresa's group, called the Missionaries of

Charity, was not yet a true religious congregation, however. Mother still needed to get the Pope's approval for her group of sisters. Her friend and spiritual advisor, Father Van Exem, helped her write the rules for the community. Finally, in 1950, Archbishop Périer traveled to Rome to present the request and all the paperwork to the Pope.

On October 7, 1950, on the feast of the Most Holy Rosary, the answer came from Rome. The Pope had approved the Missionaries of Charity! Since the congregation was new, even Mother Teresa was, under Church law, just a novice. The eleven young sisters who had joined her became postulants. The Archbishop of Calcutta would serve as superior of the congregation until Mother Teresa took her final vows as a Missionary of Charity in 1953.

"Sisters," she said, "our goal is to weave a chain of love around the whole world!"

Soon Mother Teresa's fame began to spread. More and more people heard about the work she was doing. Even people outside India began to learn of it.

Many people in many countries heard about Mother's schools, her home for the sick and dying, and her other missionary work. Donations started to come in from many different places. Bakeries sent bread, and manufacturers sent clothing. All kinds of goods, as well as money, began arriving from all over the world. All these donations were used to help the poor.

Mother and her sisters cooked stews and rice in large pots and served it to the poor of the city every day. For many of the people, these meals were their only food.

"Thank you, Mother Teresa!"

"Without you, Mother, how would we survive?"

Mother Teresa heard this every day, over and over. With a smile, she always replied, "This food came from people all over the world, from people with warm hearts. They are the ones you should thank!"

Inwardly, though, Mother was worried.

The congregation is growing so fast, and so many more young women want to join, she thought. *If only we could find a larger convent!*

Mother Teresa's prayers were answered. One day, an elderly Muslim man named Dr. Islam came to the convent.

"Mother, I have to move to another city because of my job. I have a house, a good house, but I don't need it any more. I would like to sell it to you, but at a very

low price. I received the house through God's grace, and I would like to give it back for God's work. Come and look at it."

Mother Teresa followed him and inspected the house. It was large and well located. It was in the very heart of Calcutta. It would be perfect for the Missionaries of Charity.

"Thank you, Doctor! Thank you very much, and God bless you." Mother Teresa was overjoyed!

The Archbishop of Calcutta quickly approved the purchase and advanced the money for the sale. The house became the headquarters for the Missionaries of Charity. It is still known as their "Mother House" today.

As time passed, the number of sisters and of volunteers increased. New communities of Missionaries of Charity opened in several different Indian cities. Whenever new communities opened, Mother told them:

"We must always pray and be happy to serve Jesus. When Jesus was carrying the cross, our cross, he said, 'I thirst.' What does Jesus thirst for? Is it water? Is it money? No, only our unconditional love can fulfill Jesus' thirst. The way to fulfill his thirst is by going out and finding those who are poor, abandoned, dying. We will find our beloved Jesus among them, and we will care for him. Each one of them is Christ to us."

The sisters started each day with prayer and ended with prayer. Through prayer and meditation, they received the strength and energy to help them to love and serve Jesus. Prayer was spiritual food for the Missionaries of Charity.

Chapter 7

THE PLACE OF THE PURE HEART

One day, walking on the street with another sister, Mother Teresa saw a shivering old woman wearing tattered clothes. She was lying helplessly by a rubbish heap. Mother Teresa approached her carefully. Was the woman dead?

No, she was alive, but very ill with leprosy. People were walking right by her, but no one had stopped. Surrounded by rats, and with oozing wounds, the woman was dying in front of their eyes. Mother Teresa's heart was filled with pity and sadness. She lifted the woman in her arms. Between them, she and her sister carried her to a nearby hospital.

"Sorry," the nurse told her. "There's no room for her here. She's dying, and we have to save our beds for people who can be cured. You'll just have to leave her on the streets."

Mother Teresa wasn't about to do that! She found a man who had a cart. Together they brought the woman back to the convent.

At the convent Mother prepared a bed for the woman.

"Do you have anyone to take care of you?" she asked gently. "A son, a daughter…?"

The old lady answered slowly.

"My son…is the one…who threw me on the streets."

Mother Teresa was speechless.

"I cannot forgive him," the woman whispered.

Mother Teresa said gently, "You cannot forgive him now. However, I will pray for you. You, too, must pray to God and ask him for the grace to forgive your son."

The sisters bathed the old woman, applying medicine to her sores. Soon the woman began to open her heart.

"I have lived as a beggar my whole life. So poor! So poor! My life has been worse than an animal's life, but thanks to you sisters, I am dying like an angel."

"Don't worry. We'll take care of you."

Several days later, the woman was at the point of death. The sisters prayed with her. Mother Teresa sat beside her bed.

Mother believed that every dying person should be treated with the rituals of their faith. Because this woman was a Hindu, she had asked for a little water from the Ganges River to be placed on her lips. Hindus believe water from the Ganges is holy and will help them have a peaceful death. After placing a drop of water on her lips, Mother held her hand and asked her, "My friend, are you still angry with your son?"

Tears trickled down the woman's cheeks. She shook her head.

"No, I can forgive my son now. I have learned God's love through you."

The old woman lay in Mother Teresa's arms and forgave her son. She died with a smile on her face.

After the death of the old woman, Mother Teresa was convinced more than ever that the sisters should begin a home for the dying. That evening, she told her sisters:

"All are human beings, and all should die with dignity and respect. We must care for them, wash them, and make them comfortable. That way even the poorest person can have a beautiful journey to eternal life in God."

"What can we do, Mother? How can we help?" asked the sisters.

"We must find a house for these poor rejected ones. It will be a hospice, a place where we will care for them until they die."

In the city of Calcutta, what had happened to the old woman was not uncommon. Every day, old people and even children were abandoned on the streets. Many of them were already unconscious when they were left. They suffered from starvation and disease. Thousands of people died like this in the city every year. Mother visited the city health officer, the police commissioner, and other important politicians to discuss the problem.

"Mother Teresa! We don't have enough manpower and money even to take care of the living. How are we supposed to help the dying?"

"All you need to do is provide us with a house. Our sisters will care for them with tenderness and love."

The health officer was convinced. He told his city officials, "Look for a house for Mother Teresa."

The officials looked throughout the city for a house. Several weeks later, they hadn't found one, but they'd found something else. The health officer, who was a Muslim, came to see Mother Teresa.

"Mother, we've found a place for you. However, I don't know whether you'll like it."

"Let's go see," said Mother.

The man led Mother to the Kali Temple. This was a place of worship for Hindus. It was on the banks of the Hooghly River and was visited by many pilgrims. They were people who came to pray to Kali, the Hindu goddess of death and fertility. Attached to the temple was an old building. At one time, the rooms had been used as a resting place for pilgrims. For many years, however, the rooms had been abandoned. They were empty and dirty.

Mother Teresa checked the building carefully and asked, "Are you sure it's available?"

"Yes. The temple is still used, but no one uses these rooms now. You may have the building if you want it."

"Of course, we are Catholics," Mother Teresa explained, "and don't believe in goddesses. We worship only God. But I hope the Hindus will be glad for us to use it. People used to come here to worship and rest, and now people will be able to rest here before they go to heaven. Dying people of all religions will get loving care and will be treated with respect."

Mother Teresa gratefully accepted the building. After it had been scrubbed, the sisters divided it into two separate wards, or large rooms. One was for sixty men and one for sixty women. They brought in beds and supplies. Mother and the sisters named it *Nirmal Hriday,* which means "Place of the Pure Heart."

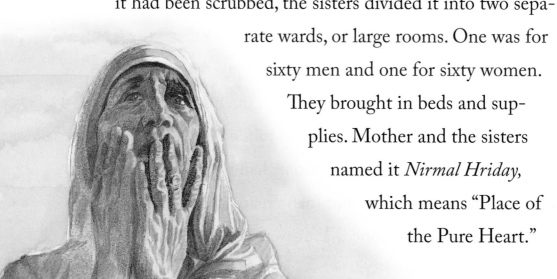

Soon dying people began to arrive.

Mother Teresa and the sisters treated them with love and compassion. Sick, filthy, and covered with sores, all could be sure of a clean bed, a warm bath, and food. Those who could not walk were brought in carts or even in wheelbarrows. In no time at all, every bed was full.

But not everyone understood the work being done by the Missionaries of Charity. Some of the local Hindu people thought that Mother Teresa was trying to convert the dying to Christianity. They were very angry. They believed that the rooms attached to the Kali Temple were being used by someone who didn't understand or respect their faith.

A group of them gathered outside Nirmal Hriday to complain.

"We can't let this go on! They should tell her to move out! The city should throw her out!"

Soon the group of angry men had grown into a mob. They began yelling insults and throwing stones at the building. As rocks thudded against the walls, Mother Teresa and all the sisters prayed silently.

Finally the men gave up.

"We'll go to the police station!" they shouted. "The police will throw her out!"

The mob milled around outside the police station, calling for the commissioner of police. Finally he appeared in the doorway.

"What's going on here? Why are you men shouting?"

"It's the Catholic woman! Why are you allowing her to take over the buildings of the Kali Temple like that? Don't you know she's got a plan to convert Hindus to Christianity? Tell her to give the place back to us!"

More and more people crowded into the area around the police station. Finally the police commissioner and a group of his officers agreed to go to Nirmal Hriday to talk to Mother Teresa.

At the hospice, Mother Teresa showed the men around. They saw how the sisters washed, clothed, and fed the dying people who had been abandoned by everyone else in the city. The commissioner saw how the sisters respected the faith of each of their dying patients. They placed water from the Ganges River on the lips of Hindus, read from the Koran for Muslims, and made sure that Catholics were given the sacrament of Anointing of the Sick.

At the end of the tour, the commissioner spoke to Mother Teresa.

"Mother, don't worry. I will solve the problem."

The commissioner left without any further questions.

When he returned to the police station, the mob of people gathered around him, shouting.

"Well, how about it? Isn't it true what we told you?"

"We should take back the building. She is defiling a holy place with her horrible, dying beggars!"

The commissioner motioned to them to be quiet. He cleared his throat and began to speak.

"As I promised you, I have inspected Mother Teresa's hospice and seen her work. It is true that she has taken in these filthy, diseased people."

The mob roared, sure that the commissioner was on their side. Finally they were going to get rid of that foreign worker and her sisters!

"There is, however, one condition before I can evict Mother Teresa from the premises," the official continued.

"Condition? What condition? Just throw her out!"

The commissioner motioned for silence. "Yes, my friends, I will certainly tell the sisters they must vacate the building. However, I cannot let those sick and dying Indian citizens be put out on the streets again. Therefore, before I evict them, I require that you must all get your mothers and sisters here to do the work these women have been doing. And of course you must help them. How does that sound?"

There was a stunned silence. How could they get their own families to take care of the dying? What was the commissioner talking about?

The official said firmly, "Listen to me, you men! In the temple is a statue of Kali, a holy goddess in stone to us, but we have a living holy person here. If you cannot do the work that Mother Teresa and her sisters are doing, then I must let them stay and continue. And that is final."

When the commissioner finished speaking, there was silence. The men realized that actions are stronger than a thousand words. Mother Teresa and her sisters were sacrificing everything to take care of the poor and dying of their city. Hindu, Muslim, or Christian, each person was taken in and allowed to die a holy death according to their faith. The men knew they had been wrong.

After that, the attitudes of people in Calcutta changed toward Mother Teresa. They understood how lucky they were to have her there. They started supporting her and her work. Today, Nirmal Hriday is still in use. Remarkably, about half of the people brought in to die actually get well. What a good thing the Missionaries of Charity weren't thrown out all those years ago!

Chapter 8

AN INSTRUMENT
OF GOD'S PEACE

Mother Teresa continued to work hard. She knew that more would have to be done to help people with leprosy. Her dream was to build a leprosy hospital. There, people could be treated, learn trades, and support themselves.

In 1957, Mother started a leprosy fund to raise money. She also declared "Leprosy Day" in Calcutta. Volunteers brought collection boxes through the city. Each had these words written on it: "Touch a leper with your kindness."

Soon a great deal of money had been donated. An ambulance was even sent from the United States. With this wonderful gift, Mother was able to begin the first of her traveling leprosy clinics. The ambulance brought medicine and doctors to areas where people had never before received health care. Because new drugs had been developed, many people with leprosy were able to get better. Some were even cured!

"In India," Mother explained, "it used to be that when you had leprosy, you were a leper for life. But now there is hope—and we can help people to recover. They can get job training and take care of themselves and their families."

Mother Teresa's next project was to build a community of houses where leprosy patients could live and work.

The Indian government donated thirty-four acres of land. Other contributions followed. Soon *Shanti Nagar*—the "Place of Peace"—became a reality.

In 1964, Pope Paul VI visited India. He traveled in a large white Lincoln Continental car. When it was time to return to Rome, he donated the car to Mother. She decided to raffle it off. The raffle made a lot of money! The profits were all donated to Shanti Nagar.

Meanwhile, in the children's home, Shishu Bhavan, hundreds of abandoned and disabled children were lovingly cared for. Some children were able to return to their families once they had regained their health and strength. Others were adopted by new families. When possible, Hindu children were adopted by Hindu parents and Christian children by Christians. Others who continued to live at Shishu Bhavan were able to attend school and receive training for jobs. Many grew up, married, and returned to visit. What joy there was when they were welcomed back!

Mother also began the Missionaries of Charity

Brothers. Brother Andrew, a young Australian priest, left the Jesuit order to become the leader of the brothers. The men worked with the sisters to provide leadership and guidance for boys. They also worked alongside them to care for the dying patients of Nirmal Hriday and the leprosy patients of Shanti Nagar. Later the brothers worked in war zones, including Vietnam and Cambodia. In 1984, Mother Teresa founded the Missionaries of Charity Fathers.

Mother knew that, by working together, the sisters, brothers, and fathers would accomplish more than each group could do alone. "Together," she said, "we can do something beautiful for God." Branches of the Missionaries of Charity have opened in over 130 countries all over the world. They are in many locations in Canada and the United States.

Over the years, Mother received many awards and honors. In 1971, she received the Pope John XXIII Peace Prize from Pope Paul VI. She was also given the Good Samaritan Award and the John F. Kennedy International

Award in the United States. Many universities through-out the world awarded her honorary degrees for her work. In 1975, she won the Albert Schweitzer International Prize.

And then, in 1979, came the most famous award of all.

One day the telephone at the convent in Calcutta rang. One of the sisters answered the phone.

"Mother Teresa, it's for you. It's someone calling from the Nobel Peace Prize committee!"

Mother came to the phone. "This is Mother Teresa speaking."

She was astonished to hear that the committee wanted to award the prize to her!

Mother was sure she wasn't worthy of such an award! Finally she agreed to accept the prize, but not for herself.

"I will accept it on behalf of all the poor," she said.

Mother Teresa traveled to Oslo, Norway, to receive the Nobel Peace Prize. The humble sister knew she would use the occasion as another chance to spread Jesus' teaching in the world.

On the night the prize was presented, Mother Teresa, in her plain white sari, stood on the stage in front of almost a thousand people. She began her speech by making the sign of the cross on her lips. She asked the audience to join with her in saying Saint Francis of Assisi's prayer for peace. This is one version of part of that prayer:

Lord, make me an instrument of your peace;

Where there is hatred,

Let me sow love;

Where there is injury, pardon;

Where there is error, truth;

Where there is doubt, faith;

Where there is despair, hope;

Where there is darkness, light;

And where there is sadness, joy.

After the prayer, Mother Teresa spoke for over an hour. She talked about her work for the poor and about the many people who had sacrificed so much to help her. Mother told her listeners that, in the face of every poor person, she saw the face of Jesus. She asked her audience to be the "Good News" of love for everyone around them. She asked each of them to become a burning light of peace in the world.

"We must start in our homes, with prayers and sacrifices," she said. "Love is born in homes!"

When Mother Teresa's speech ended, the audience gave her a standing ovation!

She had a few final words.

"Thank you for this great honor. I will spend all the award money to help the poorest of the poor."

At Mother's request, there was no big dinner held after the awards ceremony. She asked that the money that would have been spent on the dinner be donated to the poor instead. People who attended the ceremony donated even more money. With it, she was able to

feed two thousand poor people in India on Christmas Day!

There was one very special guest present at the Nobel ceremony. That was Mother Teresa's brother, Lazar. Sadly, her mother and her sister, Aga, had died in Albania years before. But how wonderful to see Lazar again!

When Mother returned to India, a large party was to be held in her honor. Many government officials and other important guests would be present. Mother Teresa asked that the party be canceled, and that the food be brought to Nirmal Hriday instead.

"Of course, Mother!" was the answer. Mother Teresa was delighted when the officials and guests even came to Nirmal Hriday to help serve the food!

After the excitement of the Nobel award, Mother Teresa wasn't able to leave the convent easily. Outside the walls, reporters and photographers from around the world crowded to see her. They all wanted to interview her and take her picture.

Mother Teresa didn't want any more publicity.

"No, no," she said. "They'll soon forget about me. I'll use the time I would have spent in answering their questions to meditate and pray instead. They'll soon go away!"

Mother Teresa was right. After a month or so, the crowds left. Soon Mother was able to leave the convent to go about her work again. For her, any time not spent in helping the poor was time wasted!

Chapter 9
HOME TO HEAVEN

When Annie returned to the Children's Home after running away, her life changed a lot. She became healthier and much happier. She went to school and worked hard to help the other children. Annie often visited Mother Teresa at the convent, and she learned all about Mother's life. She had a secret dream—to become a religious sister and join the Missionaries of Charity. Mother smiled when Annie shared this dream with her.

"Yes, of course!" she said. "Work hard and devote your life to God. With his help, we can do anything!"

What Annie didn't know was that Mother Teresa had been having problems with her health for quite a while. She first learned she had heart disease in 1983. In

1989, she suffered a heart attack, and surgeons operated to place a pacemaker in her heart. Soon after, she came down with pneumonia, which made her heart condition worse. In 1993, she fell and broke three ribs. That same year, she came down with malaria and had more heart surgery. Three years later, another fall resulted in a broken collarbone, and she had yet another heart operation.

In fact, Mother Teresa had become so ill by 1997 that she requested permission to step down as superior general of the Missionaries of Charity. It was a difficult time for everyone. No one wanted Mother to be replaced! But everyone knew she was right. She was too elderly and ill to continue in that demanding role.

Finally, on March 13, the congregation agreed that Sister Nirmala would become their new superior general. Sister Nirmala

wouldn't let anyone address her as "Mother Nirmala," though. The first time a priest tried to do it, she corrected him.

"Father, please call me 'Sister,'" she said. "We have only one Mother, and that is Mother Teresa!"

One evening in September, Annie knocked at the door of the convent to visit Mother Teresa, who had seemed very tired lately. Sister Maria let her in as usual, but where was her usual smile?

"Sister Maria, is there something wrong?" Annie asked.

The sister spoke gently. "Mother is resting, dear. She's feeling rather ill."

"Oh, Sister. Is it serious? Can I help?" asked Annie.

"You can come with me to Mother's room and say a prayer," replied the sister.

Annie knelt by Mother Teresa's bed and prayed with all her heart. Soon she slipped quietly out of the convent.

"Dear Lord," she whispered, "please bless Mother Teresa and keep her safe!"

God answered Annie's prayers in his own way. The next night, he called his faithful servant home to him in heaven. On September 5, 1997, at 9:30 PM, Mother Teresa died. She was eighty-seven years old.

Soon word of her death spread around the world. Messages of sympathy and love flooded to the convent. Pope John Paul II and many world leaders sent letters to express their sadness.

Mother Teresa's body rested in the Church of Saint Thomas More for nearly a week. During that time, the people of Calcutta were able to visit the church to see her one last time. Many came to pay their respects to "the mother to the poor." A never-ending flow of people passed her simple white casket to say goodbye.

The government of India declared that a state funeral would be held for Mother Teresa. On Saturday, September 13, her open casket, draped in the green, white, and saffron flag of India, was carried from the church by eight military officers. It was placed on a gun carriage, the same one that had been used for the funerals of

Mahatma Gandhi and Jawaharlal Nehru, two of India's great leaders. The carriage was pulled through the streets of Calcutta by a military truck. It was covered with flower wreaths and escorted by an honor guard.

Nearly a million people lined the streets. Many were weeping. From rooftops and windows, people dropped flower petals as Mother's body passed.

The procession finally arrived at the indoor sports stadium of Netaji. There, fifteen thousand people from all over the world attended Mother's three-hour funeral Mass. Important leaders from more than twenty-three countries were there. They included queens, cardinals, and presidents.

The Missionaries of Charity, however, insisted that half the seats in the stadium be reserved for the poor people of Calcutta whom Mother had so lovingly served for so many years. The eucharistic gifts of wine, water, and bread were carried to the altar by a leprosy patient, a woman just released from prison, and a disabled man.

After the Mass, Mother Teresa's body was brought home to the Mother House and buried in a simple ceremony. The sisters had a portion of the convent wall opened up to the street. Now people will always be able

to visit her grave. It has become a place of pilgrimage and prayer for people of all faiths, whether rich or poor.

Annie prays there often, along with many others. She has never forgotten the message of God's love she learned from Mother Teresa, who called it "the simple path":

The fruit of silence is PRAYER.

The fruit of prayer is FAITH.

The fruit of faith is LOVE.

The fruit of love is SERVICE.

The fruit of service is PEACE.

The Life of Mother Teresa

1910

Agnes Gonxha Bojaxhiu is born on August 26 in Sko-
pje, Macedonia, into the family of Nikola and Dranafile
Bojaxhiu. She is their third child. She has an older sister,
Aga, and a brother, Lazar.

1919

Agnes's father, Nikola Bojaxhiu, dies suddenly.

1925

As Agnes grows, she is active in parish life. She takes
part in the choir, reading groups, and the Sodality of
Children of Mary. She begins to wonder whether she

has a calling to religious life. Father Jambrekovic, the priest of her family's parish, the Church of the Sacred Heart, encourages her interest in becoming a missionary.

1928

Agnes decides to become a religious sister and joins the congregation of the Sisters of Loreto. She travels to Dublin, Ireland, for training.

1929

As a novice, Agnes arrives in Calcutta, India, with Betika Kajnc.

1931

Agnes makes her first temporary vows as a Sister of Loreto, taking the religious name of Sister Mary Teresa. From that time on, she is called Sister Teresa. She is sent to teach at Saint Mary's School, part of the sisters' Entally convent in Calcutta.

1937

Sister Teresa takes her final vows. From this point on, she is known as Mother Teresa. Soon after, she becomes principal of Saint Mary's School.

1946

Riots erupt in the streets of Calcutta as Hindus and Muslims each fight to take over the city. Thousands die in the conflict. Traveling by train to a retreat at Darjeeling, Mother Teresa hears a second inner calling from God. He tells her to leave the Loreto congregation and serve the poorest of the poor.

1948

Mother Teresa receives permission to leave the Sisters of Loreto to live and work among the poor of Calcutta. Wearing a plain white sari with blue stripes, she opens her first school in the slums of the city.

1949

Mother gives up her Yugoslavian citizenship and becomes a citizen of India.

Subhasini Das, a former student of Saint Mary's School, comes to join her. Later, other former students also join the group.

1950

The Vatican permits Mother Teresa to found a new congregation, the Missionaries of Charity.

1952

Mother Teresa opens Nirmal Hriday, a hospice for the dying, in rooms adjoining the Kali Temple.

1953

Mother takes her final vows and becomes superior of the Missionaries of Charity. The congregation moves to their new Mother House.

1954

Shishu Bhavan, a home for neglected, abandoned, and disabled children, opens in Calcutta.

1957

Shanti Nagar, a community for people living with leprosy, opens near Asansol, India.

1962

The president of India presents Mother with the Padmashri Award for distinguished service.

1963

The community of the Missionaries of Charity Brothers is established.

1965

Pope Paul VI formally appoints the Missionaries of Charity as a society of pontifical right. With the permission of the Pope,

the congregation will begin to expand into an international religious family.

Mother Teresa begins traveling frequently as the congregation opens houses in new countries.

1971

Mother Teresa is awarded the Pope John XXIII Peace Prize by the Vatican.

1972

Mother Teresa's mother, Dranafile Bojaxhiu, dies in Aran, Albania.

Mother is awarded the Nehru Prize for her promotion of international peace and understanding.

1973

Mother's older sister, Aga Bojaxhiu, dies in Tirana, Albania.

1979

Mother Teresa receives the Nobel Peace Prize in Oslo, Norway.

1980

Mother is honored with India's highest civilian award, Bharat Ratna, also known as the Jewel of India.

1982

At the height of the civil war in Beirut, Lebanon, Mother and her sisters ride in a Red Cross van to rescue thirty-seven children trapped in a hospital without food or water. Snipers from both sides hold their fire.

1983

Mother Teresa is awarded the Order of Merit by Queen Elizabeth II of England.

1984

Mother Teresa founds the Missionaries of Charity Fathers.

1985

President Ronald Reagan awards Mother Teresa with the Medal of Freedom, the highest civilian honor of the United States.

1986

Pope John Paul II visits Calcutta, India, to see and bless the work of Mother Teresa and her congregation.

1989

Mother suffers a near-fatal heart attack. She undergoes surgery and receives a pacemaker.

1990

Mother Teresa tries to resign as superior of her congregation due to her failing health. Against her wishes, however, she is re-elected as superior. She agrees to continue to serve.

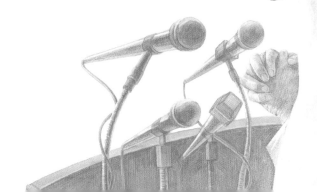

1993

Mother Teresa's long-time spiritual director and friend, Father Celeste Van Exem, dies in Calcutta.

1996

Mother Teresa is awarded honorary citizenship by the United States in recognition of her work among the poor and the sick.

Mother's health continues to worsen.

1997

Sister Agnes, the first sister to join Mother Teresa in her work for the poor in Calcutta, dies on April 9.

On September 5, Mother Teresa dies. After a state funeral, she is buried at the Mother House of the Missionaries of Charity in Calcutta.

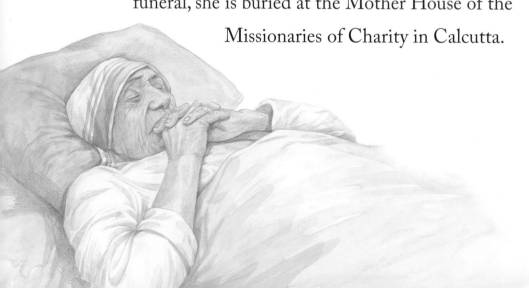

1999

Although a waiting period of at least five years is more usual, Pope John Paul II opens the cause for Mother Teresa's canonization less than two years after her death. This unusual step is due to her widespread reputation for holiness.

2003

Pope John Paul II beatifies Mother Teresa, who is now known as Blessed Teresa of Calcutta.

Glossary

Beatification—the ceremony in which the Catholic Church recognizes that a deceased person lived a life of Gospel holiness in a heroic way. In most cases, a proven miracle obtained through the holy person's prayers to God is required. A person who is beatified is given the title Blessed.

Canonization—the ceremony in which the pope officially declares that someone is a saint in heaven. To canonize someone is to recognize that he or she has lived a life of heroic virtue, is worthy of imitation, and can intercede for others. Like beatification, canonization requires a miracle resulting from the holy person's prayers to God.

Congregation (religious)—a community of men or women who live together and follow a Rule approved by the Church. They make vows of poverty, chastity, and obedience to God. The members of a congregation share a life of prayer and carry out special works of service for the good of God's people.

Convent—the name given to the house where religious sisters live.

Famine—extreme and general scarcity of food, as in a country or a large area.

Habit—the clothing that identifies a priest, brother, or sister as a member of a religious community.

Hospice—a health care facility for the dying.

Leprosy—a disease that disfigures its victims, leaving sores all over the body and causing deformities. Today it is called Hansen's disease, and it can be treated and cured.

Novice—a person in the second stage of commitment to religious life. During this time, now usually one or two years, novices grow in love for Jesus. Through prayer, study, and participation, they learn about the spirit of their congregation. They prepare to make the vows through which they will totally offer their lives to Jesus.

Pilgrim—a person who travels to a shrine or a sacred place.

Postulant— a person in postulancy, the first stage of commitment to religious life. Postulants ask to be admitted to the community as they learn what religious life will involve.

Retreat—a period of prayer and silence for the renewal of one's spiritual life.

Saffron—a bright, yellow-orange color.

Slums—crowded, rundown sections of cities where many poor people may live.

Sodality—a Catholic organization whose members perform charitable or spiritual works.

Superior—the title given to the person who governs and serves a religious community.

Vocation—a call from God to a certain way of life. A person may have a vocation to the married life, the priesthood, the religious life, or the single life. Everyone has a vocation to be holy.

Vow—an important promise freely made to God. Members of religious communities usually make vows of poverty, chastity, and obedience. Missionaries of Charity also make a vow of wholehearted and free service to the poorest of the poor.

Ready to Read More?

The *Encounter the Saints* series offers intermediate readers down-to-earth portrayals of the saints. Each story vividly recreates for the reader the saint's place of origin, family life, and corresponding historical events.

Blessed Teresa of Calcutta
Missionary of Charity
Mary Kathleen Glavich, SND
Mother Teresa dedicated her life to helping the poorest of the poor in India. Here is the inspiring life story of this Nobel Peace Prize winner, respected and beloved worldwide.
Paperback   136pp.
#11602 $7.95 ($9.95 Cdn)

Saint Martin de Porres
Humble Healer
Elizabeth Marie DeDomenico, FSP
Brother Martin was "only" a humble friar in Peru—but this gentle saint used his healing skills to care for people of all races and nationalities. Discover why the story of Saint Martin is still so relevant today!
Paperback   120pp.
#70919 $7.95 ($9.95 Cdn)

Saint Katharine Drexel
The Total Gift
Susan Helen Wallace, FSP
The inspiring story of the Philadelphia heiress who gave her life to Jesus and spent her huge fortune helping others. This second U.S.-born saint founded the Sisters of the Blessed Sacrament to serve Native and African-Americans.
Paperback   144pp.
#70684 $7.95 ($9.95 Cdn)

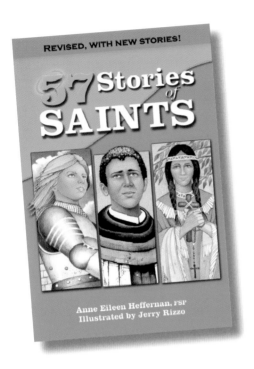

57 Stories of Saints
Revised, with New Stories
Anne Eileen Heffernan, FSP;
illustrated by Jerry Rizzo
Some of the best-loved saints of
the Church are featured in a revised
and updated edition of a classic
collection. Wonderfully written
biographies and illustrations of
Saints Lucy, Monica, Augustine,
Benedict, Francis Xavier, Edith
Stein, Juan Diego, Katharine Drexel,
and many others.
Paperback   544pp.
#26812 $16.95 ($21.25 Cdn)

Holy Friends
Thirty Saints and Blesseds
  of the Americas
Diana M. Amadeo; illustrated by
Irina Lombardo with Augusta Curreli
Features saints and blesseds from the
American continents in a beautifully
illustrated hardcover book. Each
story includes a quotation from the
saint, as well as a concluding prayer.
Hardcover   138pp.
#33843 $19.95 ($24.95 Cdn)

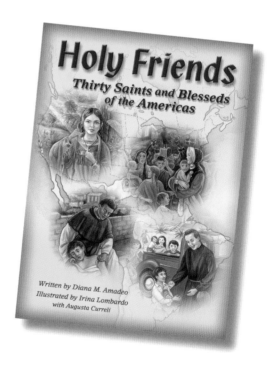

Pauline
BOOKS & MEDIA

The Daughters of St. Paul operate book and media centers at the following addresses. Visit, call or write the one nearest you today, or find us on the World Wide Web, www.pauline.org

CALIFORNIA
3908 Sepulveda Blvd, Culver City, CA 90230   310-397-8676
2640 Broadway Street, Redwood City, CA 94063   650-369-4230
5945 Balboa Avenue, San Diego, CA 92111   858-565-9181

FLORIDA
145 S.W. 107th Avenue, Miami, FL 33174   305-559-6715

HAWAII
1143 Bishop Street, Honolulu, HI 96813   808-521-2731
Neighbor Islands call: 866-521-2731

ILLINOIS
172 North Michigan Avenue, Chicago, IL 60601   312-346-4228

LOUISIANA
4403 Veterans Memorial Blvd, Metairie, LA 70006   504-887-7631

MASSACHUSETTS
885 Providence Hwy, Dedham, MA 02026   781-326-5385

MISSOURI
9804 Watson Road, St. Louis, MO 63126   314-965-3512

NEW JERSEY
561 U.S. Route 1, Wick Plaza, Edison, NJ 08817   732-572-1200

NEW YORK
150 East 52nd Street, New York, NY 10022   212-754-1110

PENNSYLVANIA
9171-A Roosevelt Blvd, Philadelphia, PA 19114   215-676-9494

SOUTH CAROLINA
243 King Street, Charleston, SC 29401   843-577-0175

TENNESSEE
4811 Poplar Avenue, Memphis, TN 38117   901-761-2987

TEXAS
114 Main Plaza, San Antonio, TX 78205   210-224-8101

VIRGINIA
1025 King Street, Alexandria, VA 22314   703-549-3806

CANADA
3022 Dufferin Street, Toronto, ON M6B 3T5   416-781-9131